THE SMALL STAKES
MUSIC POSTERS

THE SMALL STAKES MUSIC POSTERS
BY
JASON MUNN

FOREWORD BY NICHOLAS HARMER,
DEATH CAB FOR CUTIE

CHRONICLE BOOKS
SAN FRANCISCO

Library of Congress Cataloging-in-Publication Data is available.

ISBN 978-0-8118-7230-0

Manufactured in China.
Design by Jacob T. Gardner and Jason Munn
Typeset in Gotham

10 9 8 7 6 5 4 3 2

Chronicle Books LLC
680 Second Street
San Francisco, CA 94107
www.chroniclebooks.com

This book is dedicated to the endless number of bands that have been the source of my inspiration. Without them these pages would be blank. I am forever grateful.

JASON MUNN

FOREWORD
BY NICHOLAS HARMER

BASSIST, DEATH CAB FOR CUTIE

I'll admit that design was not a big priority during the early years of our band. Sure, we were aware of it, but certainly the idea of consciously designing a "look" for our music seemed very antithetical to our beliefs about where our music was coming from and how we wanted to be known. We eschewed fashion, were shy about photographs, and held our DIY work ethic close to our hearts. Sure, we always wanted to make our albums look and sound great, but the idea of a specific band font or logo to develop a "look"? Not in a million years. The music would speak for itself. So we just kept our heads down and did the things we knew we could do: record albums and play shows. Everything else, we figured, would happen naturally. Good people, we hoped, would find each other.

As I reflect on those years, it feels like there had to be some invisible hand guiding us to Jason. We didn't seek him out any more than he sought us out; he was a friend of a friend who, like us, was just getting things started. In the beginning, he made a poster for one show. What we didn't know was that the venue for that particular show prohibited their name being printed on posters created by outside designers. Consequently, Jason had to remove the venue name, leaving us both with a stack of posters not really announcing anything except some band names. On a whim, we decided that we would sell these posters at our merchandise table to help Jason recoup the printing costs. Just like that we had our first ever tour poster. And they sold like hotcakes. So we asked for more designs. And that's how one poster turned into more posters, a wide selection of band merchandise, artwork for a live EP, and eventually our first Web site. The timing was everything: we were growing and beginning to reach a large audience, and Jason's designs organically became the "look" of our band as we made it on to more and more radars.

What worked then about Jason's designs still works today. I still marvel at his sense of what isn't needed. His work is not overstuffed, crowded, or noisy. And I identify with his humble lack of showiness. I know my band works at these qualities too. We have always done our best to not be overtly showy, on stage or on record. In the studio we constantly reference our unofficial working creed: less is more. As in, just because I can play a dramatic fill on my bass, or display some musical flash, it doesn't mean I should. Sometimes, one note can say more than twenty. When I look at Jason's work, I see the same mechanism at play. I see an understated elegance to what he makes, to the juxtapositions and compositions he chooses. This is why I feel like our music and Jason's designs still make a perfect pairing—we complement the simplicity in each other.

I know I could go on and on about what draws me to Jason's work and how amazing it has been to see us both continue to grow over the years. But really, for me, the greatest thing about our relationship is that our earliest belief held true: good people, did in fact, find each other. I'd sure like to shake that invisible hand and say thanks for making the introduction.

NICHOLAS HARMER

INTERVIEW
JAY RYAN AND JASON MUNN

When the rock poster community figured out which way was up, gained momentum, and reached a sort of critical mass in 2002, some of the dirty uncles of the new scene threw out an open invitation to come to a big convention style event in San Francisco to show work and meet each other. We were surprised when "Flatstock," as it was called, attracted a crowd of people who knew exactly what they were anxiously coming to see, and another crowd of people who had no idea what to expect.

Jason Munn came to this first Flatstock convention as a spectator, recognized that this is where he belonged, and took the initiative to show up the next year with an impressive new portfolio of his own work. Now, six years later, he is well liked and well respected in this community, and his work is a constant source of inspiration and frustration for me (I envy his clarity and precision). His work doesn't seek to be cool or funny or naughty like so much of the work I see. Jason touches on traditions of good design and shows a sense of economy and restraint that is lacking in much of today's visual world.

JAY RYAN
The Bird Machine, a Chicago-based print shop

I like to think of you as the guy who came to the first Flatstock in San Francisco as a spectator, having never made a poster, who thought, "I can do that," went home, and was at the top of the field a year later.

JASON MUNN: I was very much inspired by going to the first Flatstock. Going in and seeing the work of Jeff Kleinsmith and Factor 27 and your work in person pretty much solidified that this was something I wanted to do. I had done a few album packages and T-shirt designs for friends of mine in bands, but I didn't have any idea about how to go beyond that. Leaving that first Flatstock, I knew I wanted to start making posters, but I just didn't have a real clear idea on how.

RYAN: You were working at a T-shirt shop around the time you started making posters. Were you printing before you started making posters, or were the two linked?

MUNN: I was doing temp work at a T-shirt shop in Oakland soon after I moved from Wisconsin. I wasn't doing any printing but had a basic knowledge on how to screen print. Around this same time some friends of mine asked me to create posters to advertise shows for this venue they started booking bands at. The venue was called The Ramp and was located in the basement of a church in Berkeley.

The shows were typically a couple local bands, with a touring band. Deerhoof, Damien Jurado, Animal Collective, Why?, and Danielson were some of the bands that played at The Ramp during its far-too-short existence of one year.

I was really excited about this and agreed to design the posters, but I was a little unsure about how we would get them produced. I decided the best way to get them produced was to screen print them, since we were only creating around fifty for each show. These early posters were printed from home, but I would get my screens burned at the T-shirt shop where I worked.

RYAN: At what point did you decide that making posters, specifically, was your thing, as opposed to doing general design, or whatever? Was there a "eureka" moment, or did you just end up gradually working, until posters were all that you were working on?

MUNN: After doing a few posters for The Ramp, I was pretty hooked. During this time, I started doing other posters for bands playing in San Francisco that I knew or had met through The Ramp. I was still working part-time and doing temp work during this period while also spending a fair amount of time looking for a full-time job at a design studio.

For a while I felt I was right in between being able to officially go out on my own or continue to look for a job at another studio. This was about the time that I got one of my first commissions from Death Cab for Cutie: a set of tour posters and some T-shirt designs.

RYAN: It seems to me like you have been specifically good at finding the core, the main theme of the subject matter, and depicting that in a clear way, without pandering. By pandering, I mean that you keep the visual dialogue intelligent, and keep it as an in-joke for those who know the band.

MUNN: When I start creating a poster, my goal is to make something that feels appropriate for the band. I don't always feel that I reach this, but regardless it's the goal. There is always a fine line between creating work that feels appropriate and also feels like your own in some way.

RYAN: You reach a clear balance, that way, clearer than I've ever been able to. You don't stand in the way of the subject matter like I do, or some other people can. Egoless design?

MUNN: There are a few different ways I look at it. Overall, I am really attracted to bodies of work. On one hand, I have always been drawn to artists who have a particular style that has developed over years, like your work. There is this consistency that I really respect. The best way I know how to try and keep the work consistent over time is to keep doing work that feels appropriate for the bands.

RYAN: And yet, it retains obvious personality. It's clearly a "Jason Munn print," most of the time.

MUNN: Thanks. I've been trying to experiment a little more with some of the recent work. Trying to expand on the direct and simple graphics I typically do. Still keeping the designs appropriate for the bands, but leaving them a little more open ended. I've been enjoying and struggling with pushing the designs in some new directions. Occasionally, when a poster makes me nervous at first, it will later be one of my favorites or a bit of a turning point.

RYAN: I see a bit of a turn to abstraction, such as in the recent Antony and the Johnsons and Deerhunter prints. You also started making your own images, as opposed to using found images, a few years ago, right?

MUNN: Yeah, the Antony and Deerhunter prints are definitely a bit different for me, but I'm also still trying to make something that seems suitable and, in my mind, looks how the band sounds. Bands like Deerhunter that feel more experimental in nature lead me to designs that are more experimental. The Deerhunter poster in particular has been one of my favorite posters over the last year or so.

My work has gone through a few phases. A lot of my early poster designs were collage based, combing various found imagery to communicate my ideas. I would also occasionally reinterpret or reference ephemeral images, like an old record cover or advertisement that inspired me. Manipulating and changing familiar or found imagery was definitely part of my growth as a designer. My designs in general have gotten simpler over the years, but I think stronger. I still occasionally use some found imagery or textures along with my own additions to complete a design.

RYAN: As far as pushing what you're doing, does scale ever come into question? Pretty much 100 percent of your work has been within a few inches of 18 by 24, right?

MUNN: Most everything is 18 by 24 inches. A lot of the older posters were 19 by 25 because that was the size of the paper as it was when it arrived. I've been sticking to the 18-by-24 size for the past few years—I've been happy keeping that consistency. Having those limitations actually helps my design process and keeps a consistency throughout the work. That being said, I recently had the chance to create a film poster for a showing of the film created by The Flaming Lips called *Christmas On Mars*, and those posters were 24 by 36 inches. I would definitely like to explore larger formats more as well as more film posters.

RYAN: Ever think about doing the work you do, but as paintings? Drawings? Is it the image making, or the fact that you're working with your favorite musicians? Is poster making an act of being a fan of the music, or does it serve the purpose of putting meaning behind images you feel would otherwise be meaningless?

MUNN: Ultimately, what gets me working is the idea of solving a problem or creating something for subject matter I'm excited about. I've realized I do need to have that meaning behind the images and, oftentimes, a deadline. A lot of my images are so specific to the bands that I often can't imagine the images being on their own.

RYAN: How has your process changed over time?

MUNN: My overall design process hasn't changed much over the years. I approach the overall process in much the same way as I did when I started, typically spending more time in the concept stages versus in front of the computer. Learning to screen print and printing my own work for the first five years has shaped the way I design more than anything. Understanding my limitations as a printer steered the way I was designing.

RYAN: So the process became part of the design. I understand that you are no longer printing most of your work.

MUNN: Most of my work is printed by Nat Swope of Bloom Screen Printing. Soon after I started printing my own work, I met Nat and showed him some of my posters. For me, the whole act of making posters was all over the place at first. I was just starting to design in the format but also learning how to print at the same time. After I showed Nat some of my work, he began to help me out with a lot of questions and problems I was having with printing. He would look at my prints and start seeing where I was having trouble. Soon after that, I started printing out of his shop, and that has been one of the main constants in getting my work produced. Nat has always printed the larger jobs that I couldn't print, and he now prints most of my work. This has always brought a consistency to my work that I've been happy with. Seeing the other work that Nat was printing in his shop also led me to learn a lot about printing and utilize these aspects in my own designs. Since Nat has been printing most of my work over the past year, it has opened up my thinking a bit.

RYAN: "I couldn't do this, but maybe he can"?

MUNN: Exactly. He also provides a fair amount of input. I can send him a mock-up of something I'm working on, and he can make a suggestion from a printer's point of view.

RYAN: Do you feel like you're appealing to any particular traditions in design?

MUNN: Yes, I do, but it is somewhat haphazard. I didn't study design history, but over the past couple of years I've begun to learn a lot more and actually draw more inspiration from it. I've learned about design history somewhat by looking at contemporary designers and going backwards, so to speak. What really appeals to me is a lot of the mid-twentieth-century design work: clean lines; restrained, organized typography; and the limited use of color.

RYAN: You just go day to day for the most part, but if you had to leap ahead, what do you see yourself doing when you're 53?

MUNN: I do think about this, sometimes too much. As you said, I just try to go day to day, but I am also thinking about where the work can be headed on a larger scale, although I don't want to get hung up on this as well. I always hope that over time the work will naturally change and move in different directions and build off of my previous work. What I'm doing combines my two obsessions: design and music.

PEDRO THE LION, 2002
WITH SELDOM AND SCIENTIFIC
Two-color silk screen, 19 × 25 inches

PINBACK W/ HELLA • THE GREAT AMERICAN MUSIC HALL DEC. 16
DOORS 7:30 SHOW 8:00 • $13 ADVANCE $15 DOOR

PINBACK, 2002
WITH HELLA
Three-color silk screen, 19 × 25 inches

DAMIEN JURADO, 2003
WITH ROCKY VOTOLATO AND ADAM VOITH
Two-color silk screen, 19 × 25 inches

ASPECTS OF PHYSICS, 2003
WITH SAXON SHORE AND MAP
Two-color silk screen, 19 × 25 inches

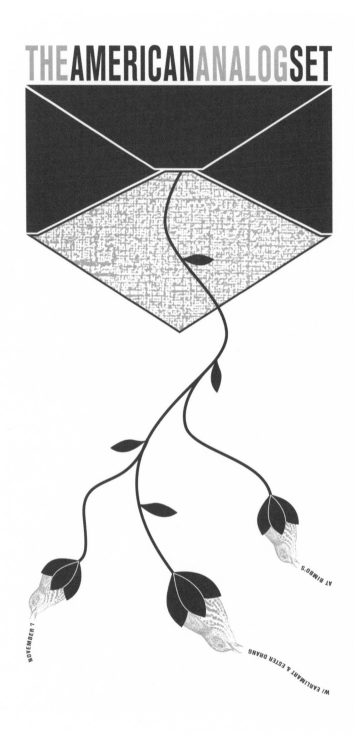

THE AMERICAN ANALOG SET, 2003
WITH EARLIMART AND ESTER DRANG
Two-color silk screen, 19 × 25 inches

THE AMERICAN ANALOG SET

WINTER TOUR 2003 W/ THE ALBUM LEAF

12.03
DALLAS
12.04
NEW ORLEANS
12.05
ATLANTA
12.06
CARRBORO
12.08
ORLANDO
12.09
WEST PALM BEACH
12.10
TAMPA
12.11
GAINESVILLE
12.12
MT. PLEASANT
12.13
CHATTANOOGA
12.15
WASHINGTON D.C.
12.16
PHILADELPHIA
12.17
NEW YORK
12.18
BURLINGTON
12.19
CAMBRIDGE

THE AMERICAN ANALOG SET, 2003
WINTER TOUR WITH THE ALBUM LEAF
Two-color silk screen, 19 × 25 inches

ALKALINE TRIO, 2003
WITH ONE MAN ARMY, THE START, AND PARIS TEXAS
Two-color silk screen, 19 x 25 inches

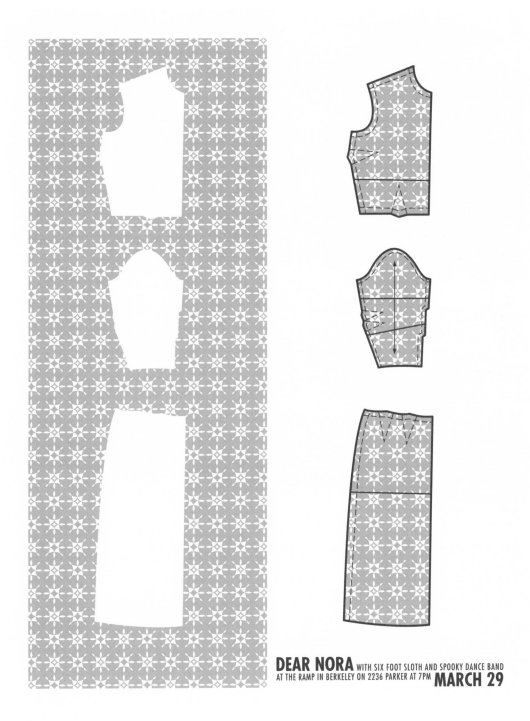

DEAR NORA WITH SIX FOOT SLOTH AND SPOOKY DANCE BAND
AT THE RAMP IN BERKELEY ON 2236 PARKER AT 7PM **MARCH 29**

DEAR NORA, 2003
WITH SIX FOOT SLOTH AND SPOOKY DANCE BAND
Two-color silk screen, 19 × 25 inches

LES SAVY FAV, 2003
Two-color silk screen, 19 × 25 inches

LUNGFISH, 2003
SPRING TOUR
One-color silk screen, 19 × 25 inches

10.09.03 | W/ THE THERMALS + ROGUE WAVE | 10.10.03 | W/ I AM THE WORLD TRADE CENTER + NIK FREITAS | BOTTOM OF THE HILL | 18 + | $12

MATES OF STATE, 2003
WITH THE THERMALS, ROGUE WAVE, I AM THE WORLD TRADE CENTER, AND NIK FREITAS
Three-color silk screen, 19 × 25 inches

MATES OF STATE AND RAINER MARIA, 2003
WITH LOQUAT AND DEAR NORA
Two-color silk screen, 19 × 25 inches

PEDRO THE LION, 2003
WITH THE STRATFORD 4, STARFLYER 59, AND ESTER DRANG
Two-color silk screen, 19 × 25 inches

TED LEO AND THE PHARMACISTS, 2003
WITH THE COST AND COMMUNIQUE
Two-color silk screen, 19 × 25 inches

Q AND NOT U • 9.28.03 • W/ BLACK EYES & ANTELOPE • BOTTOM OF THE HILL • 9PM

Q AND NOT U, 2003
WITH BLACK EYES AND ANTELOPE
Two-color silk screen, 19 × 25 inches

Q AND NOT U, 2003
WITH ENGINE DOWN AND ROCKY VOTOLATO
Two-color silk screen, 19 × 25 inches

THE DISMEMBERMENT PLAN, 2003
WITH ENON AND BEAUTY PILL
Two-color silk screen, 19 × 25 inches

AGAINST ME!, 2003
WITH FIFTH HOUR HERO
Two-color silk screen, 19 × 25 inches

WHY? WITH CRIME IN CHOIR AND THE MOORE BROTHERS W/ NEDELLE AT THE RAMP ON AUGUST 17TH AT 7PM FOR 6 DOLLARS

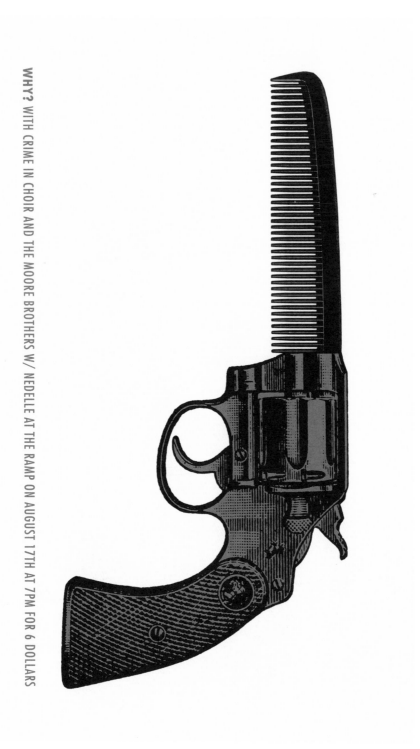

WHY?, 2003
WITH CRIME IN CHOIR AND THE MOORE BROTHERS WITH NEDELLE
Two-color silk screen, 12.5 x 19 inches

NUMBERS, 2003
WITH TRIN TRAN AND COACHWHIPS
Two-color silk screen, 12.5 x 19 inches

ASTAIRE, 2004
Two-color silk screen, 18 × 24 inches

BEULAH, 2004
Two-color silk screen, 19 × 25 inches

DEATH CAB FOR CUTIE, 2004
FALL TOUR
Three-color silk screen, 19 × 25 inches

NORTH AMERICAN TOUR FALL 2004

9/28 BOSTON, MA • 9/29 BOSTON, MA • 10/1 READING, PA • 10/2 TOLEDO, OH • 10/3 GRAND RAPIDS, MI

10/5 ST. LOUIS, MO • 10/6 ASHEVILLE, NC • 10/8 KISSIMMEE, FL • 10/10 FORT LAUDERDALE, FL • 10/11 TAMPA, FL

10/12 ATLANTA, GA • 10/13 COLUMBUS, OH • 10/14 CHICAGO, IL • 10/15 KANSAS CITY, MO • 10/16 MINNEAPOLIS, MN

10/17 PONTIAC, MI • 10/19 BOSTON, MA • 10/20 PHILADELPHIA, PA • 10/21 PROVIDENCE, RI • 10/22 NEW YORK, NY

10/23 WASHINGTON, DC • 10/24 CARRBORO, NC • 10/25 CARRBORO, NC • 10/26 NASHVILLE, TN • 10/28 NEW ORLEANS, LA

10/29 HOUSTON, TX • 10/30 AUSTIN, TX • 10/31 FT. WORTH, TX • 11/2 LAS VEGAS, NV • 11/3 SAN DIEGO, CA

11/4 POMONA, CA • 11/5 LOS ANGELES, CA • 11/6 SAN FRANCISCO, CA • 11/7 SPARKS, NV • 11/8 CHICO, CA

11/9 SEATTLE, WA • 11/10 PORTLAND, OR • 11/12 VANCOUVER, BC

DEATH CAB FOR CUTIE, 2004
FALL TOUR WITH DATES
Two-color silk screen, 19 × 25 inches

BEN KWELLER AND DEATH CAB FOR CUTIE, 2004
SPRING TOUR
Two-color silk screen, 19 × 25 inches

DEATH CAB FOR CUTIE AND BEN KWELLER, 2004
SPRING TOUR
Two-color silk screen, 19 × 25 inches

HOT SNAKES
OCTOBER 3 • W/ TROUBLE EVERYDAY & THE HUSBANDS
GREAT AMERICAN MUSIC HALL • 8PM • $14 • ALL AGES

HOT SNAKES, 2004
WITH TROUBLE EVERYDAY AND THE HUSBANDS
Three-color silk screen, 19 × 24.5 inches

FEBRUARY 26 W/ JOLIE HOLLAND   NOISE POP 2004   GREAT AMERICAN MUSIC HALL

LOW, 2004
WITH JOLIE HOLLAND
Two-color silk screen, 19 × 25 inches

IRON & WINE, 2004
WITH HOLOPAW AND PATRICK MCKINNEY
Two-color silk screen, 19 × 25 inches

WITH THE LIARS • NOVEMBER 16 & 17 • BIMBO'S 365 CLUB

BLONDE REDHEAD, 2004
WITH LIARS
Two-color silk screen, 19 × 25 inches

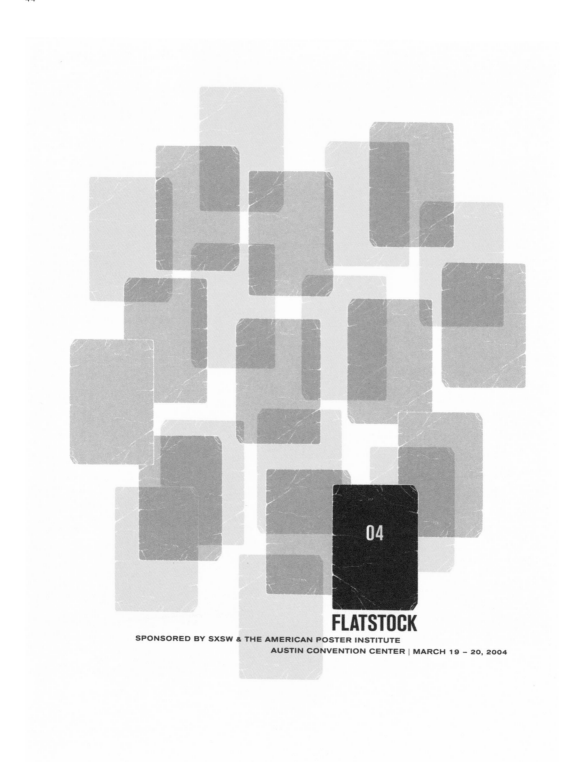

FLATSTOCK, 2004
Three-color silk screen, 19 x 25 inches

THE DECEMBERISTS, 2004
WITH EARLIMART AND THE RUM DIARY
Two-color silk screen, 19 x 25 inches

NOVEMBER 18 STATE THEATRE **NOVEMBER 20** FOX THEATRE   **NOVEMBER 22** STATE THEATRE **DETROIT**

PIXIES, 2004
Three-color silk screen, 19 × 25 inches

CAT POWER, 2004
WITH WOMEN AND CHILDREN AND MT. EGYPT
Three-color silk screen, 18 × 24.5 inches

W/ NOW IT'S OVERHEAD & TILLY AND THE WALL **SEPTEMBER 23** BIMBO'S 365 CLUB   EIGHTEEN AND OVER

RILO KILEY, 2004
WITH NOW IT'S OVERHEAD AND TILLY AND THE WALL
Three-color silk screen, 19 × 24.5 inches

SUFJAN STEVENS, 2004
WITH JOANNA NEWSOM, DENISON WITMER, AND HALF-HANDED CLOUD
Two-color silk screen, 18 × 24 inches

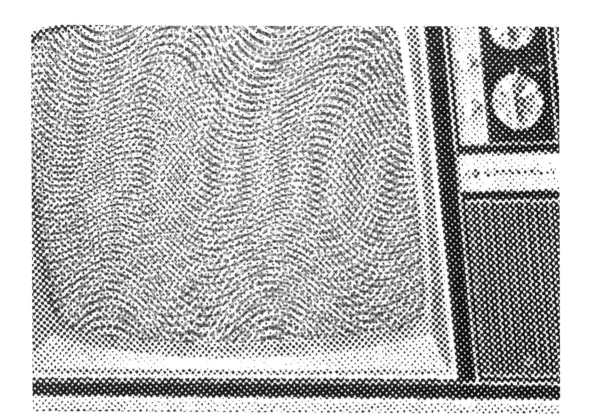

W/ BEANS AND THE ETERNALS | JUNE 1 | BIMBOS 365 CLUB

TORTOISE, 2004
WITH BEANS AND THE ETERNALS
Three-color silk screen, 18 × 24 inches

WILCO, 2004
Three-color silk screen, 18.5 × 25 inches

GREAT AMERICAN MUSIC HALL
FEBRUARY 27 **PEDRO THE LION** NOISE POP 2004
W/ JOHN VANDERSLICE & ESTER DRANG

PEDRO THE LION, 2004
WITH JOHN VANDERSLICE AND ESTER DRANG
Two-color silk screen, 19 × 25 inches

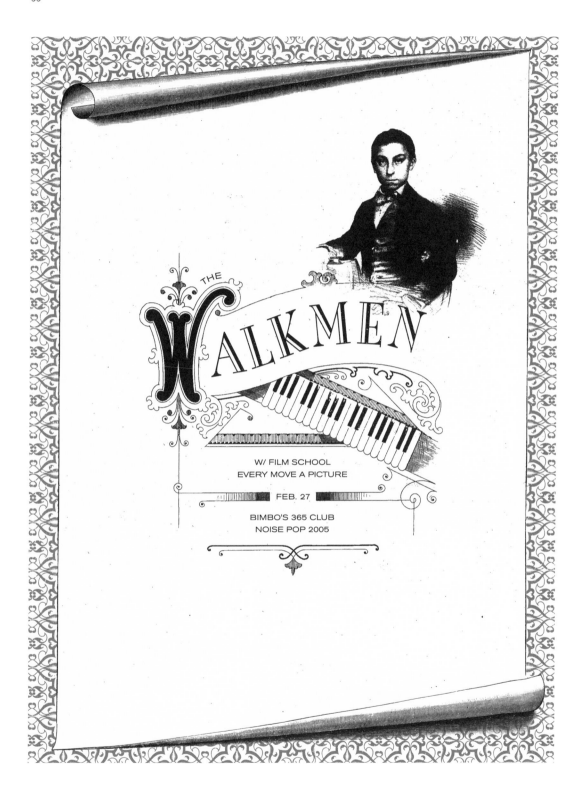

THE WALKMEN, 2005
WITH FILM SCHOOL AND EVERY MOVE A PICTURE
Two-color silk screen, 18 × 24 inches

DEATH CAB FOR CUTIE, 2005
HURRICANE KATRINA BENEFIT CONCERT WITH HARVEY DANGER
Two-color silk screen, 19 × 25 inches

GREAT AMERICAN MUSIC HALL
WITH FOREIGN BORN AND MAZARIN
DECEMBER 18, 2005

ROGUE WAVE, 2005
WITH FOREIGN BORN AND MAZARIN
Three-color silk screen, 19 × 25 inches

PERFORMING AT THE SASQUATCH! MUSIC FESTIVAL

JOANNA NEWSOM

SATURDAY, MAY 28, 2005 | MEMORIAL DAY WEEKEND | THE GORGE | TICKETS AT TICKETMASTER | PRODUCED BY HOUSE OF BLUES

WWW.SASQUATCHFESTIVAL.COM

JOANNA NEWSOM, 2005
Two-color silk screen, 19 × 25 inches

WITH OCTIS | GREAT AMERICAN MUSIC HALL | NOVEMBER 21

ANIMAL COLLECTIVE, 2005
WITH OCTIS
Two-color silk screen, 19 × 25 inches

HOTEL S N'S   1625 N. MOZART   CHICAGO, IL
JANUARY 29, 2005 · INVITATION ONLY

JEFF TWEEDY, 2005
Two-color silk screen, 19 × 25 inches

FEIST, 2005
WITH JOHN VANDERSLICE, YOUTH GROUP, AND THE BOTTICELLIS
Two-color silk screen, 19 × 25 inches

STARS, 2005
WITH APOSTLE OF HUSTLE AND FEIST
Three-color silk screen, 19 × 25 inches

BUILT TO SPILL, 2005
WITH STEVEN WRAY LOBDELL AND APE SHAPE
Four-color silk screen, 18 x 24.5 inches

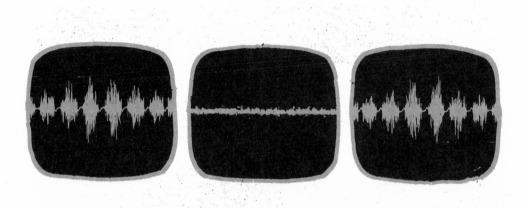

MISSION OF BURMA, 2005
WITH ERASE ERRATA AND THE RUBY DOE
Two-color silk screen, 19 × 25 inches

NADA SURF, 2005
WITH THE VELVET TEEN, GOLDEN REPUBLIC, AND THE WINECHUGGERS
Three-color silk screen, 19 × 25 inches

THE AMERICAN ANALOG SET, 2005
TENTH ANNIVERSARY SHOW
Two-color silk screen, 19 × 25 inches

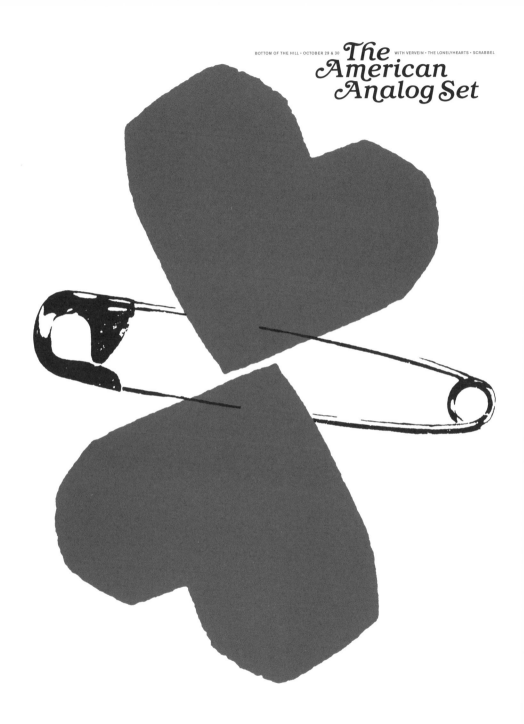

BOTTOM OF THE HILL · OCTOBER 29 & 30 · WITH VERVEIN · THE LONELYHEARTS · SCRABBEL

The American Analog Set

THE AMERICAN ANALOG SET, 2005
WITH VERVEIN, THE LONELYHEARTS, AND SCRABBEL
Two-color silk screen, 19 × 25 inches

stellastarr*
the metro
september 13

STELLASTARR*, 2005
HARMONIES FOR THE HAUNTED RECORD RELEASE (CHICAGO)
Two-color silk screen, 18 x 24 inches

stellastarr*
irving plaza new york city
october 6 stellastarr.com

STELLASTARR*, 2005
HARMONIES FOR THE HAUNTED RECORD RELEASE (NEW YORK)
Two-color silk screen, 18 × 24 inches

SUFJAN STEVENS, 2005
WITH DANIELSON FAMILE, BUNKY, SMOOSH, CASTANETS,
FEATHERS, LIZ JANES, AND HALF-HANDED CLOUD
Two-color silk screen, 19 × 25 inches

SUFJAN STEVENS AND THE ILLINOISEMAKERS, *2005*
WITH LAURA VEIRS AND LIZ JANES
Two-color silk screen, 18 × 24 inches

DECEMBER 2
PARCHMAN FARM • THE DECORATION
SLIM'S

THE WRENS, 2005
WITH PARCHMAN FARM AND THE DECORATION
Two-color silk screen, 18 × 24 inches

CASTANETS, 2005
FIRST LIGHT'S FREEZE ALBUM RELEASE
Two-color silk screen, 18 × 24 inches

PRODUCED BY HOUSE OF BLUES CONCERTS

KINGS OF LEON
– AND –
SECRET MACHINES

PORTLAND • FRIDAY **JULY 15** • TICKETSWEST.COM
SEATTLE • SATURDAY **JULY 16** • TICKETMASTER.COM
EUGENE • SUNDAY **JULY 17** • TICKETSWEST.COM

KINGS OF LEON AND SECRET MACHINES, 2005
Two-color silk screen, 18.5 x 24.5 inches

2006
SPRING/SUMMER TOUR

JOSH
RITTER

NEW ALBUM
THE ANIMAL YEARS
OUT NOW

JOSH RITTER, 2006
SPRING-SUMMER TOUR
Two-color silk screen, 18 x 24 inches

BROKEN SOCIAL SCENE

MANCHESTER ACADEMY FEBRUARY 14 £8.50

RGG107 WWW.RICHARDGOODALLGALLERY.COM

BROKEN SOCIAL SCENE, 2006
Two-color silk screen, 18 × 24 inches

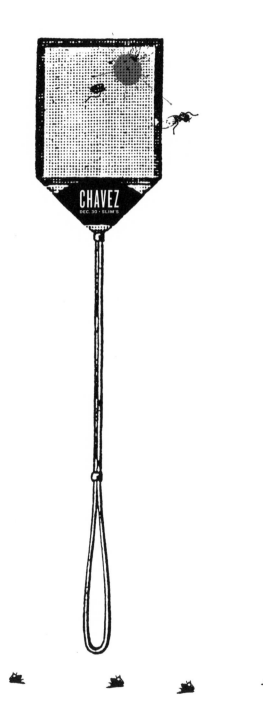

CHAVEZ, 2006
Two-color silk screen, 18 × 24 inches

CLAP YOUR HANDS SAY YEAH (Front), 2006
WITH THE BRUNETTES
Two-color silk screen, 18 × 24 inches

MARCH 24 AND 25 GREAT AMERICAN MUSIC HALL W/ THE BRUNETTES

CLAP YOUR HANDS SAY YEAH (Back), 2006
WITH THE BRUNETTES
Two-color silk screen, 18 × 24 inches

NEKO CASE, 2006
WITH SONNY SMITH
Two-color silk screen, 19 × 25 inches

Presented by House of Blues Concerts

with Special Guest **ERIC BACHMANN**

JUNE 21 SHOWBOX 9PM

Tickets are available online at ticketswest.com or hob.com, all Ticketswest outlets, including Rudy's Barbershops and select QFC Food Centers. Charge by phone at (800) 325-7328.

CALEXICO, 2006
WITH ERIC BACHMANN
Two-color silk screen, 19 × 25 inches

BONNIE "PRINCE" BILLY, 2006
WITH DARK HAND AND LAMPLIGHT AND SIR RICHARD BISHOP
Two-color silk screen, 18 × 24 inches

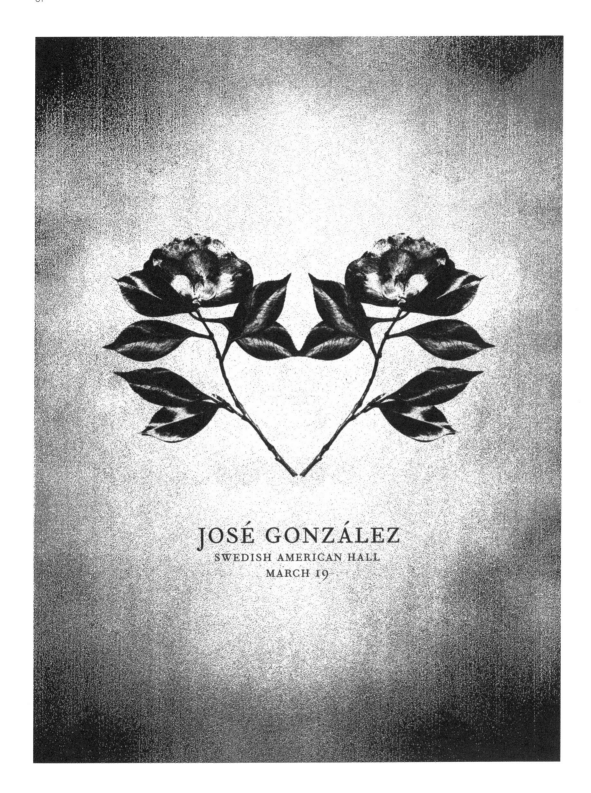

JOSÉ GONZÁLEZ, 2006
Two-color silk screen, 18 × 24 inches

JOSH RITTER, 2006
FALL TOUR
Two-color silk screen, 18 × 24 inches

AUGUST 11 & 12

DEATH CAB FOR CUTIE

W/ SPOON & MATES OF STATE

TWO SHOWS • THE GREEK THEATRE • BERKELEY

DEATH CAB FOR CUTIE, 2006
WITH SPOON AND MATES OF STATE
Three-color silk screen, 18 × 25 inches

Mates of State

with VIVA VOCE and THE BOTTICELLIS

GREAT AMERICAN MUSIC HALL

April 28, 2006

MATES OF STATE, 2006
WITH VIVA VOCE AND THE BOTTICELLIS
Two-color silk screen, 19 × 25 inches

NOVEMBER 21 & 22, 2006

MATES**OF**STATE

THE COURT & SPARK · STILL FLYIN' · ASOBI SEKSU · THE BOTTICELLIS

GREAT AMERICAN MUSIC HALL

MATES OF STATE, 2006
WITH THE COURT & SPARK, STILL FLYIN', ASOBI SEKSU, AND THE BOTTICELLIS
Two-color silk screen, 18 × 24 inches

THE SHINS, 2006
Two-color silk screen, 19 × 25 inches

MY BRIGHTEST DIAMOND, 2006
BRING ME THE WORKHORSE CD RELEASE SHOW
Two-color silk screen, 19 × 25 inches

THE CONSTANTINES, 2006
WITH OAKLEY HALL AND BRILLIANT RED LIGHTS
Two-color silk screen, 19 × 25 inches

NOUVELLE VAGUE
FALL TOUR 2006

9/3	Seattle, WA	Bumbershoot
9/5	Vancouver, BC	Plaza Nightclub
9/6	Portland, OR	Doug Fir Lounge
9/7	San Francisco, CA	Fillmore
9/8	Los Angeles, CA	Henry Fonda Theater
9/10	Salt Lake City, UT	Urban Lounge
9/11	Englewood, CO	Gothic Theatre
9/13	Chicago, IL	Metro
9/14	Toronto, ON	The Mod Club
9/15	Montreal, PQ	Club Soda
9/16	Boston, MA	Paradise
9/17	Phildelphia, PA	World Café
9/19	New York, NY	Webster Hall
9/20	Washington, DC	Embassy of France
9/21	Atlanta, GA	Variety Playhouse
9/22	Orlando, FL	The Social
9/23	Miami, FL	Studio A

NOUVELLE VAGUE, 2006
FALL TOUR
Two-color silk screen, 19 × 25 inches

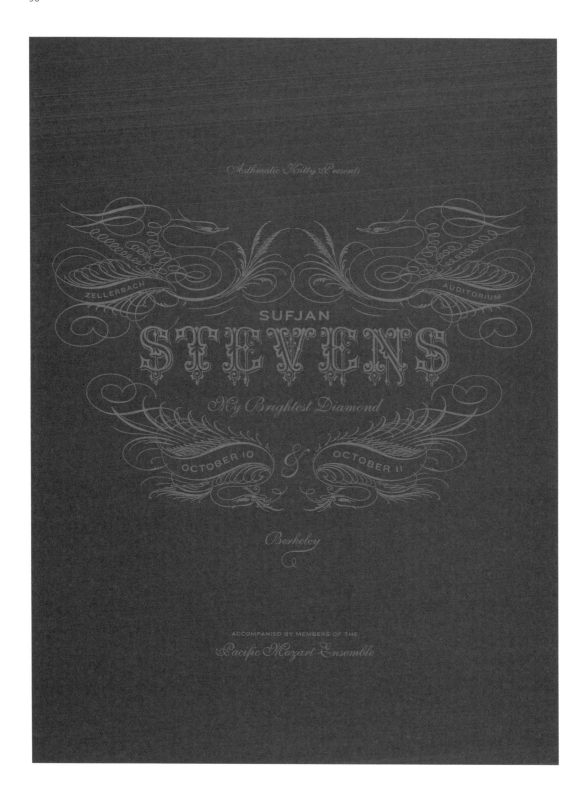

SUFJAN STEVENS, 2006
WITH MY BRIGHTEST DIAMOND
One-color silk screen, 18 × 24 inches

TAG TEAM MEDIA FIFTH ANNIVERSARY, 2006
WITH BROKEN SOCIAL SCENE
Two-color silk screen, 19 × 25 inches

MATT POND PA
W/ DIOS (MALOS)

NEW YORK BOSTON PROVIDENCE MONTREAL TORONTO DETROIT CLEVELAND PITTSBURGH
CINCINNATI COLUMBUS INDIANAPOLIS CHICAGO MINNEAPOLIS MADISON
ST. LOUIS LAWRENCE DENVER SALT LAKE CITY BOISE
WINTER TOUR 2006

MATT POND PA, 2006
WINTER TOUR WITH DIOS (MALOS)
Two-color silk screen, 18.5 × 25 inches

MATT POND PA, 2006
WINTER TOUR WITH YOUTH GROUP
Two-color silk screen, 18.5 × 25 inches

THE WALKMEN, 2006
WITH MAZARIN AND SIMON DAWES
Three-color silk screen, 19 × 25 inches

SAN FRANCISCO MUSEUM of MODERN ART
PRESENTS COLLEGE NIGHT WITH NOISE POP

FEATURING REX RAY, PARADISE BOYS, AND JIMMY TAMBORELLO

SEPTEMBER 21, 2006
6-9PM

SAN FRANCISCO MUSEUM OF MODERN ART, COLLEGE NIGHT, 2006
WITH REX RAY, PARADISE BOYS, AND JIMMY TAMBORELLO
Two-color silk screen, 19 × 25 inches

THE BOOKS, 2006
WITH CLOGS
Two-color silk screen, 19 × 25 inches

THE BOOKS, 2007
WITH TODD REYNOLDS
Two-color silk screen, 18 × 24 inches

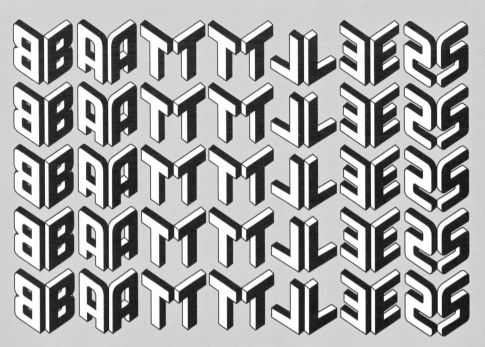

NOVEMBER 1 / GREAT AMERICAN MUSIC HALL / with NO AGE

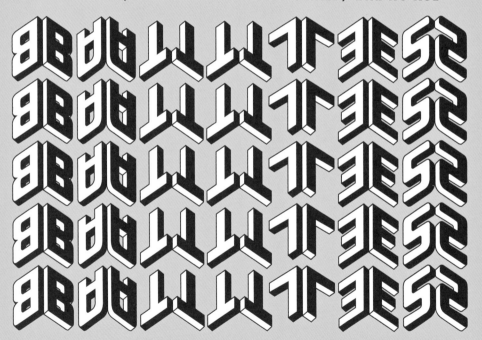

BATTLES, 2007
WITH NO AGE
Two-color silk screen, 18 × 24 inches

BEN GIBBARD, 2007
SPRING TOUR WITH DAVID BAZAN AND JOHNATHAN RICE
Two-color silk screen, 18 × 24 inches

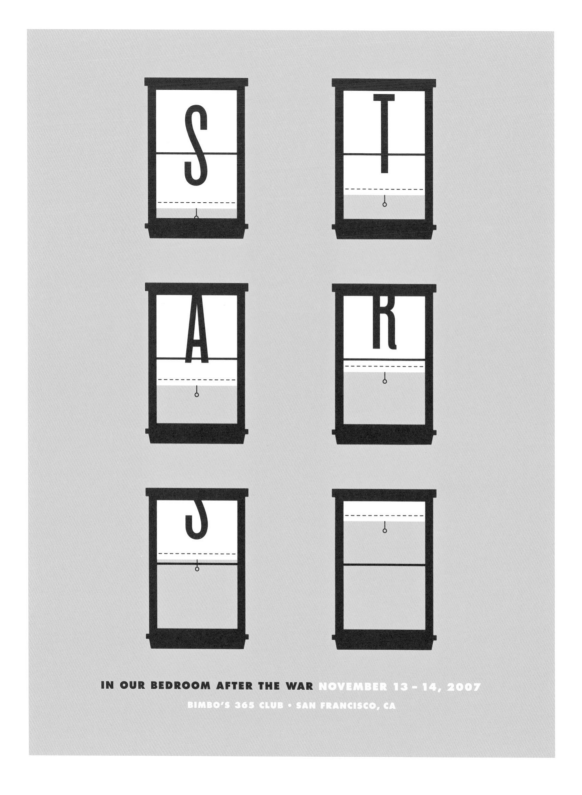

STARS, 2007
IN OUR BEDROOM AFTER THE WAR, SAN FRANCISCO
Two-color silk screen, 18 × 24 inches

BEN HARPER, 2007
LIFELINE RECORD RELEASE
Two-color silk screen, 18 × 24 inches

CAMERA OBSCURA, 2007
WITH PORTASTATIC
Two-color silk screen, 18 × 24 inches

BRIGHT
EYES

VETIVER • ANNIE STELA • PORT O'BRIEN

GREAT AMERICAN MUSIC HALL
MARCH 9 - 10, 2007

BRIGHT EYES, 2007
WITH VETIVER, ANNIE STELA, AND PORT O'BRIEN
Two-color silk screen, 18 × 24 inches

MARK KOZELEK, 2007
FALL EUROPEAN TOUR
Two-color silk screen, 18 × 24 inches

MARK KOZELEK, 2007
LONDON
Two-color silk screen, 18 × 24 inches

DANIEL JOHNSTON, 2007
WITH THE OHSEES
Two-color silk screen, 18 × 24 inches

LOW
SEPTEMBER 25 & 26, 2007
GREAT AMERICAN MUSIC HALL
W/ AZALIA SNAIL & CHARLIE PARR

LOW, 2007
WITH AZALIA SNAIL AND CHARLIE PARR
Two-color silk screen, 18 × 24 inches

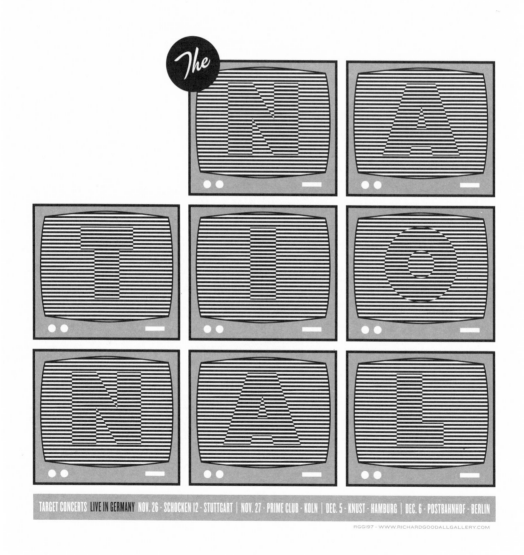

THE NATIONAL, 2007
GERMAN TOUR
Two-color silk screen, 18 × 24 inches

LCD SOUNDSYSTEM, *2007*
SOUND OF SILVER RECORD RELEASE
Two-color silk screen, 18 × 24 inches

THE NATIONAL, 2007
WITH THE BROKEN WEST
Two-color silk screen, 18 × 24 inches

THE DECEMBERISTS, 2007
Two-color silk screen, 18 × 24 inches

NOISE POP AND ANOTHER PLANET ENTERTAINMENT PRESENT

TREASURE ISLAND MUSIC FESTIVAL

MODEST MOUSE • SPOON • BUILT TO SPILL • THIEVERY CORPORATION • GOTAN PROJECT • M.I.A. • KINKY
DJ SHADOW & CUT CHEMIST • CLAP YOUR HANDS SAY YEAH • AU REVOIR SIMONE • ZION I • M.WARD
TWO GALLANTS • GHOSTLAND OBSERVATORY • FLOSSTRADAMUS • SEA WOLF • EARLIMART
DEVIL MAKES THREE • STREET TO NOWHERE • TRAINWRECK RIDERS • FILM SCHOOL
DENGUE FEVER • HONEYCUT • WEST INDIAN GIRL • MOCEAN WORKER • KID BEYOND

SEPTEMBER 15 & 16, 2007

TREASURE ISLAND MUSIC FESTIVAL, 2007
Two-color silk screen, 18 × 24 inches

THE SHINS, 2007
Three-color silk screen, 18 × 24 inches

MAY 1, 2007
EXPLOSIONS IN THE SKY
W/ ELUVIUM | SLIM'S

EXPLOSIONS IN THE SKY, 2007
WITH ELUVIUM
Three-color silk screen, 18 × 24 inches

MODEST MOUSE WITH MAN MAN ⚓ NOVEMBER 30, 2007 ⚓ KZOO STATE THEATRE

MODEST MOUSE, 2007
WITH MAN MAN
Two-color silk screen, 18 × 24 inches

MODEST MOUSE, 2007
WITH MATT COSTA
Two-color silk screen, 18 × 24 inches

NORAH JONES, 2007
WITH M. WARD
Two-color silk screen, 18 × 24 inches

GOMEZ
— AND —
BEN KWELLER

MARCH 8 AND 9 | WEBSTER HALL
NYC

GOMEZ AND BEN KWELLER, 2007
Two-color silk screen, 18 × 24 inches

NOISE POP MUSIC FESTIVAL, 2007
FIFTEENTH ANNIVERSARY POSTER
Two-color silk screen, 18 × 24 inches

BLONDE REDHEAD
with ANNUALS | APRIL 23 and 24, 2007 | BIMBO'S 365 CLUB

BLONDE REDHEAD, 2007
WITH ANNUALS
Two-color silk screen, 18 × 24 inches

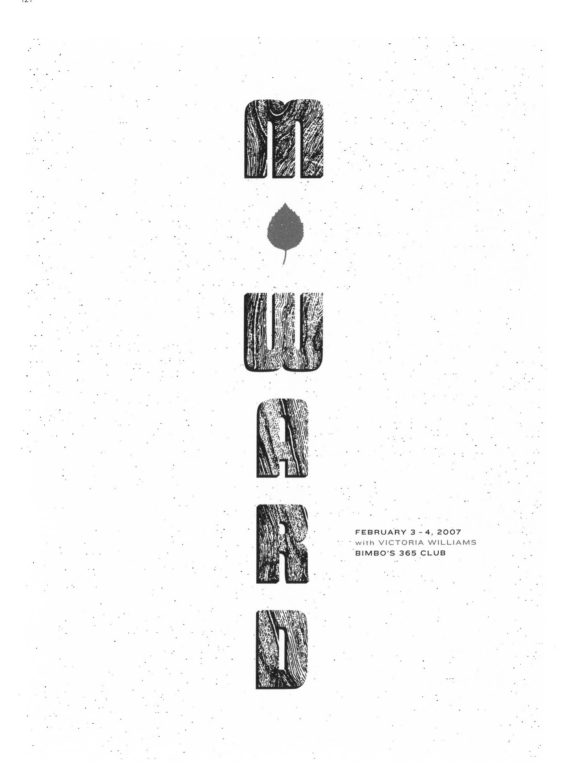

FEBRUARY 3 - 4, 2007
with VICTORIA WILLIAMS
BIMBO'S 365 CLUB

M. WARD, 2007
WITH VICTORIA WILLIAMS
Two-color silk screen, 18 × 24 inches

STARS, 2007
IN OUR BEDROOM AFTER THE WAR, U.S. TOUR
Two-color silk screen, 18 x 24 inches

STARS, 2007
IN OUR BEDROOM AFTER THE WAR, CANADIAN TOUR
Two-color silk screen, 18 x 24 inches

STARS, 2007
IN OUR BEDROOM AFTER THE WAR, PHOENIX CONCERT THEATRE
Two-color silk screen, 18 × 24 inches

STARS, 2008
IN OUR BEDROOM AFTER THE WAR, EUROPEAN TOUR
Two-color silk screen (glows in the dark), 18 × 24 inches

BUILT TO SPILL

Performing
PERFECT FROM NOW ON
SEPTEMBER 8, 2008 · SLIM'S
with **QUASI** and **OFF CAMPUS**

BUILT TO SPILL PERFORMING PERFECT FROM NOW ON (First Night), 2008
WITH QUASI AND OFF CAMPUS
Two-color silk screen, 18 × 24 inches

Performing
PERFECT FROM NOW ON
SEPTEMBER 9, 2008 · SLIM'S
with **QUASI** and **OFF CAMPUS**

BUILT TO SPILL PERFORMING PERFECT FROM NOW ON (Second Night), 2008
WITH QUASI AND OFF CAMPUS
Two-color silk screen, 18 × 24 inches

D E
E R
H U N
T E R

NOVEMBER 24

with TIMES NEW VIKING

GREAT AMERICAN MUSIC HALL

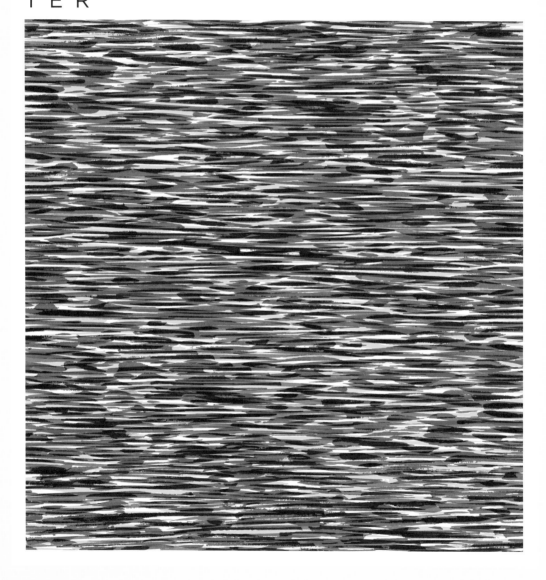

DEERHUNTER, 2008
WITH TIMES NEW VIKING
Four-color silk screen, 18 × 24 inches

EXPLOSIONS IN THE SKY with LICHENS | MARCH 20 • 21 • 22, 2008 | GREAT AMERICAN MUSIC HALL

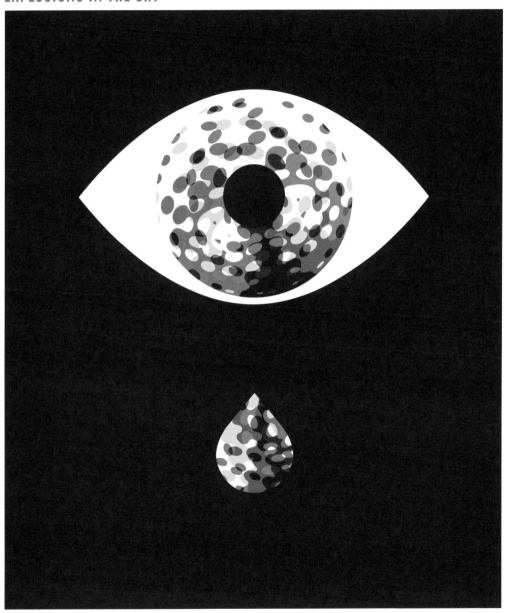

EXPLOSIONS IN THE SKY, 2008
WITH LICHENS
Four-color silk screen, 18 × 24 inches

BECK

AUSTIN CITY LIMITS MUSIC FESTIVAL
SEPTEMBER 27, 2008

BECK, 2008
AUSTIN CITY LIMITS MUSIC FESTIVAL
Four-color silk screen, 18 × 24 inches

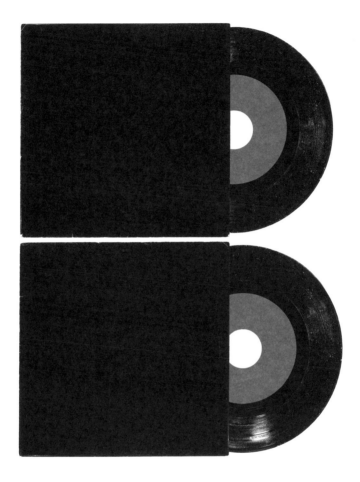

BECK, 2008
WITH DAN THE AUTOMATOR
Two-color silk screen, 18 × 24 inches

CONSTANTINES

CONSTANTINES, 2008
INSOUND 20 SERIES
Two-color silk screen, 18 × 24 inches

DEATH CAB FOR CUTIE, 2008
INSOUND 20 SERIES
Two-color silk screen, 18 × 24 inches

THE NEW PORNOGRAPHERS, 2008
INSOUND 20 SERIES
Four-color silk screen, 18 × 24 inches

GRIZZLY BEAR, 2008
INSOUND 20 SERIES
Two-color silk screen, 18 × 24 inches

BEIRUT, 2008
INSOUND 20 SERIES
Three-color silk screen, 18 × 24 inches

CALEXICO, 2008
INSOUND 20 SERIES
Three-color silk screen, 18 × 24 inches

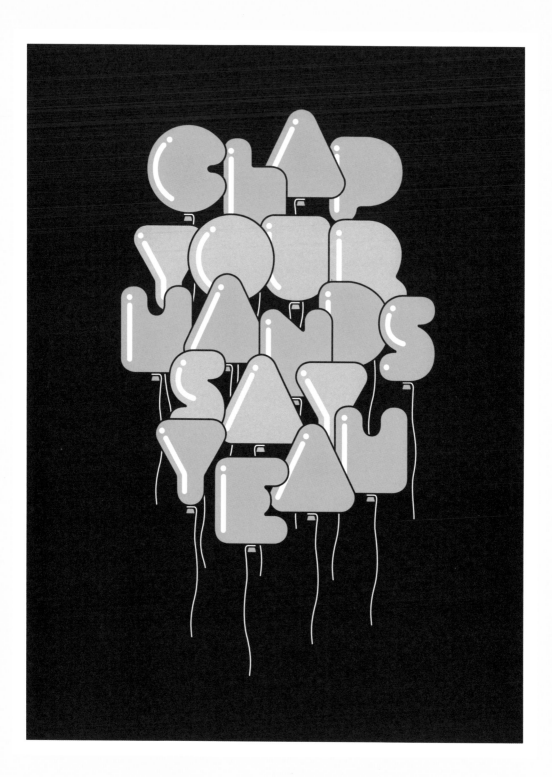

CLAP YOUR HANDS SAY YEAH, 2008
INSOUND 20 SERIES
Three-color silk screen, 18 × 24 inches

THE THERMALS, 2008
INSOUND 20 SERIES
Three-color silk screen, 18 × 24 inches

JOSÉ GONZÁLEZ

JOSÉ GONZÁLEZ, 2008
INSOUND 20 SERIES
Three-color silk screen, 18 × 24 inches

PETER BJORN and JOHN

PETER BJORN AND JOHN, 2008
INSOUND 20 SERIES
Two-color silk screen, 18 × 24 inches

MAGNOLIA ELECTRIC CO., 2008
INSOUND 20 SERIES
Two-color silk screen, 18 × 24 inches

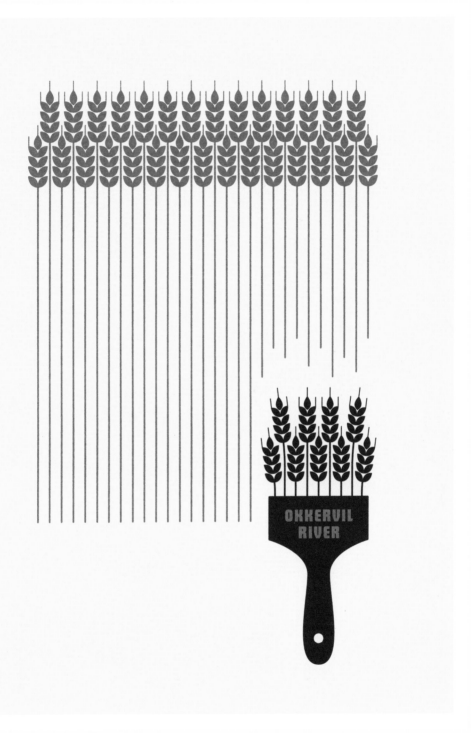

OKKERVIL RIVER, 2008
INSOUND 20 SERIES
Three-color silk screen, 18 × 24 inches

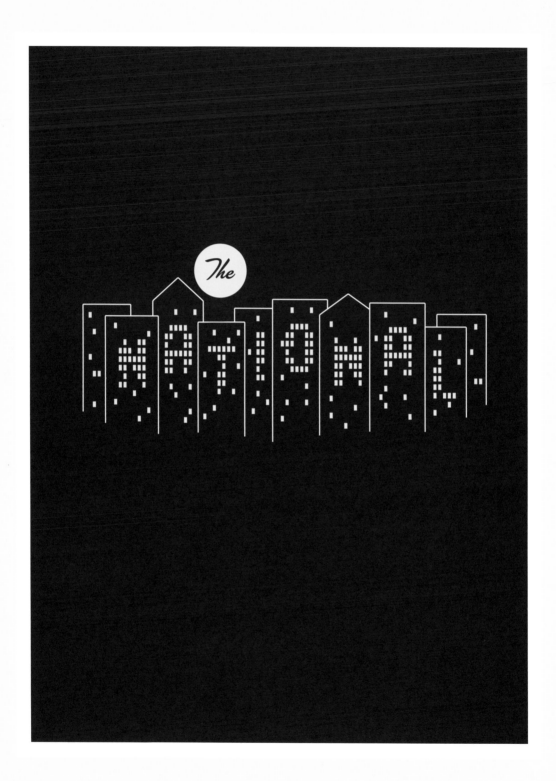

THE NATIONAL, 2008
INSOUND 20 SERIES
Two-color silk screen, 18 × 24 inches

DEPARTMENT OF EAGLES

DEPARTMENT OF EAGLES, 2008
INSOUND 20 SERIES
Two-color silk screen, 18 × 24 inches

THE DECEMBERISTS, 2008
INSOUND 20 SERIES
Three-color silk screen, 18 × 24 inches

SPOON, 2008
INSOUND 20 SERIES
Three-color silk screen, 18 × 24 inches

SHE & HIM

SHE & HIM, 2008
INSOUND 20 SERIES
Two-color silk screen, 18 × 24 inches

THE HOLD STEADY, 2008
INSOUND 20 SERIES
Three-color silk screen, 18 × 24 inches

BUILT TO SPILL, 2008
INSOUND 20 SERIES
Three-color silk screen, 18 × 24 inches

THE BLACK HEART PROCESSION, 2008
INSOUND 20 SERIES
Two-color silk screen, 18 × 24 inches

JENS LEKMAN with THE HONEYDRIPS on MARCH 22, 2008 at BIMBO'S 365 CLUB

JENS LEKMAN, 2008
WITH THE HONEYDRIPS
Two-color silk screen, 18 × 24 inches

EUROPEAN TOUR 2008

SUN KIL MOON

STOCKHOLM • MALMÖ • ANTWERP • PARIS • BRIGHTON
MANCHESTER • BIRMINGHAM • NORTH DORSET
GLASGOW • NOTTINGHAM • LONDON
BRISTOL • DUBLIN

SUN KIL MOON, 2008
EUROPEAN TOUR
Two-color silk screen, 18 × 24 inches

NADA SURF, 2008
Two-color silk screen, 18 × 24 inches

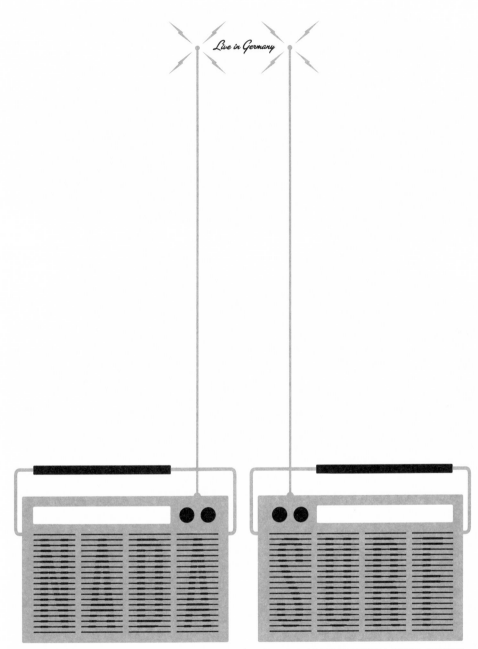

NADA SURF, 2008
GERMAN TOUR
Two-color silk screen, 18 × 24 inches

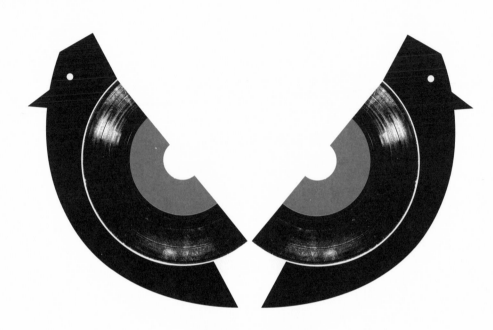

THE NATIONAL, 2008
TOUR POSTER
Two-color silk screen, 18 × 24 inches

ALOPECIA
RECORD RELEASE

MARCH 6, 2008 | DOSE ONE + CRYPTACIZE + ODD NOSDAM + JEL | GREAT AMERICAN MUSIC HALL | PRESENTED BY PERFORMER

WHY?, 2008
WITH DOSE ONE, CRYPTACIZE, ODD NOSDAM, AND JEL
Two-color silk screen, 24 × 18 inches

THE MAGNETIC FIELDS, 2008
WITH INTERSTELLAR RADIO COMPANY
Two-color silk screen, 18 × 24 inches

MARK KOZELEK, 2008
SPRING-SUMMER TOUR
Two-color silk screen, 18 × 24 inches

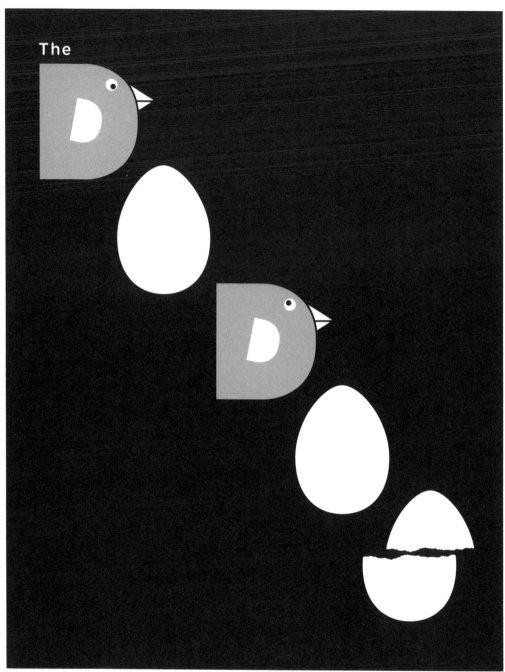

The

THURSDAY, NOVEMBER 6, 2008 | with KELLY STOLTZ | BIMBO'S 365 CLUB

THE DODOS, 2008
WITH KELLY STOLTZ
Two-color silk screen, 18 x 24 inches

NOVEMBER 2 & 3, 2008   **SHE & HIM**   BIMBO'S 365 CLUB • 18+

with LAVENDER DIAMOND

SHE & HIM, 2008
WITH LAVENDER DIAMOND
Two-color silk screen, 18 × 24 inches

CHRISTMAS ON MARS, 2008
Three-color silk screen, 24 x 36 inches

THIS IS SPINAL TAP, 2009
Two-color silk screen, 24 × 36 inches

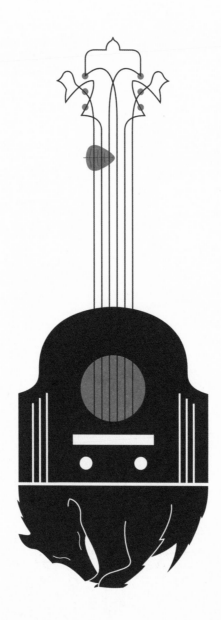

JOSH RITTER SOLO ACOUSTIC EDITIONS

GOLDEN AGE OF RADIO | HELLO STARLING | THE ANIMAL YEARS

JOSH RITTER, 2009
SOLO ACOUSTIC EDITIONS PROMOTIONAL POSTER
Two-color silk screen, 18 x 24 inches

MONSTERS OF FOLK, 2009
Two-color silk screen, 18 x 24 inches

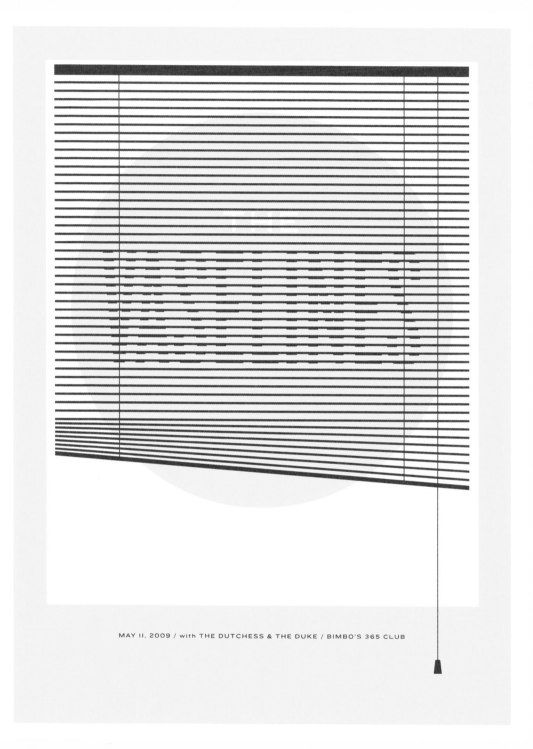

MAY II, 2009 / with THE DUTCHESS & THE DUKE / BIMBO'S 365 CLUB

THE VASELINES, 2009
WITH THE DUTCHESS AND THE DUKE
Two-color silk screen, 18 x 24 inches

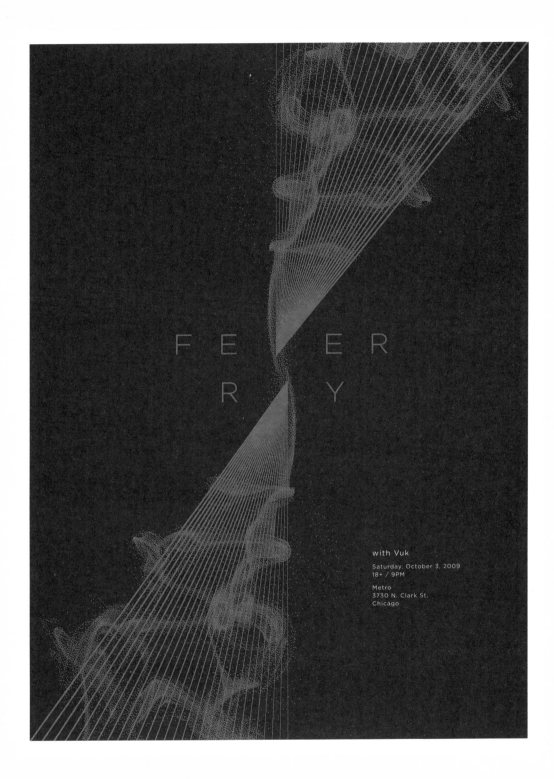

FEVER RAY, 2009
WITH VUK
Two-color silk screen, 18 × 24 inches

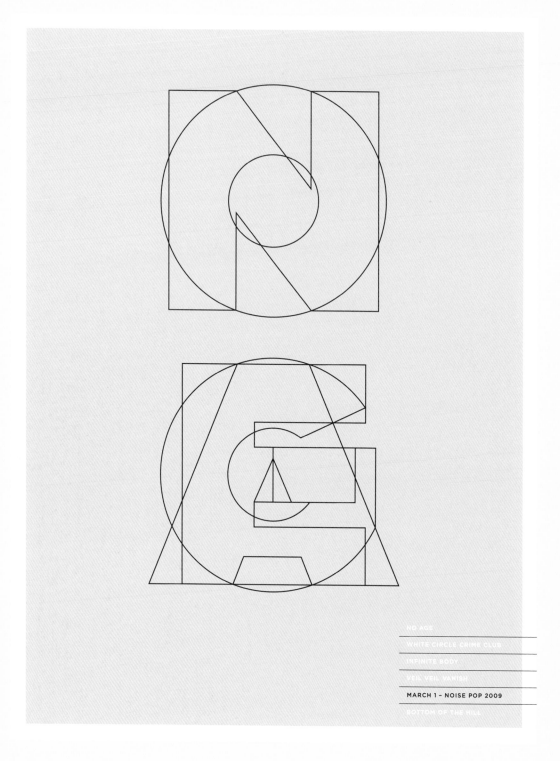

NO AGE, 2009
WITH WHITE CIRCLE CRIME CLUB, INFINITE BODY, AND VEIL VEIL VANISH
Two-color silk screen, 18 × 24 inches

A. C. **NEWMAN** W/ THE BROKEN WEST · MARCH 29, 2009 · THE BELL HOUSE · BROOKLYN, NEW YORK

A. C. NEWMAN, 2009
WITH THE BROKEN WEST
Two-color silk screen, 18 × 24 inches

WHY? October 17, 2009 / with Mount Eerie, Au, and Serengetti & Polyphonic / Great American Music Hall

WHY?, 2009
WITH MOUNT EERIE, AU, AND SERENGETTI & POLYPHONIC
Three-color silk screen, 18 x 24 inches

May 21, 2009 / High Noon Saloon / Madison, WI

SCHOOL OF
SEVEN BELLS

BLACK MOTH
SUPER RAINBOW

SCHOOL OF SEVEN BELLS AND BLACK MOTH SUPER RAINBOW, 2009
Four-color silk screen, 18 × 24 inches

Antony and the Johnsons

ANTONY AND THE JOHNSONS, 2009
Three-color silk screen, 18 x 24 inches

THE TALLEST MAN ON EARTH

with Red Cortez / Saturday, April 11, 2009

The Brattle Theatre / Cambridge, MA

THE TALLEST MAN ON EARTH, 2009
WITH RED CORTEZ
Three-color silk screen, 18 × 24 inches

APRIL 24, 2009 / with THE TWILIGHT SAD / CAT'S CRADLE / CARRBORO, NC

MOGWAI, 2009
WITH THE TWILIGHT SAD
Four-color silk screen, 18 × 24 inches

antony and the johnsons

saturday, february 28, 2009

the moore theatre

tickets and info www.stgpresents.org

ANTONY AND THE JOHNSONS, 2009
Two-color silk screen, 18 × 24 inches

Andrew Bird with Loney Dear | February 27, 2009 | Slowdown | Omaha, NE

ANDREW BIRD, 2009
WITH LONEY DEAR
Three-color silk screen, 18 × 24 inches

FLIGHT OF THE CONCHORDS, 2009
WITH ARJ BARKER
Two-color silk screen, 18 × 24 inches

ANDREW BIRD

with St. Vincent
Sunday, October 25, 2009
Electric Factory / Philadelphia, PA

ANDREW BIRD, 2009
WITH ST. VINCENT
Five-color silk screen, 18 × 24 inches

THE ECHO FALLS

THE ECHO FALLS, 2009
ALBUM RELEASE POSTER
Two-color silk screen, 18 × 24 inches

Bill Callahan

June 30, 2009 / with Bachelorette / Bimbo's 365 Club

BILL CALLAHAN, 2009
WITH BACHELORETTE
Two-color silk screen, 18 × 24 inches

SONIC YOUTH

JULY 24, 2009 / with AWESOME COLOR
KNITTING FACTORY / SPOKANE, WA

SONIC YOUTH, 2009
WITH AWESOME COLOR
Four-color silk screen, 18 × 24 inches

WEST COAST   # SUN KIL MOON   SPRING 2009

May 21, Wonder Ballroom, Portland | May 23, Sasquatch Festival, Seattle | May 27, El Rey Theatre, Los Angeles | May 29, Great American Music Hall, San Francisco

SUN KIL MOON, 2009
WEST COAST SPRING TOUR
Three-color silk screen, 18 × 24 inches

MARK KOZELEK

July 18, Tonsberg, Norway / July 19, London, UK / July 20, Manchester, UK / July 21, Colchester, UK

July 23, Dublin, Ireland / July 25, Giske, Norway / August 6, Brooklyn, New York

August 9, Myslowice, Poland / August 11, Moscow, Russia / August 14, St. Malo, France

SUMMER TOUR 2009

MARK KOZELEK, 2009
SUMMER TOUR
Two-color silk screen, 18 × 24 inches

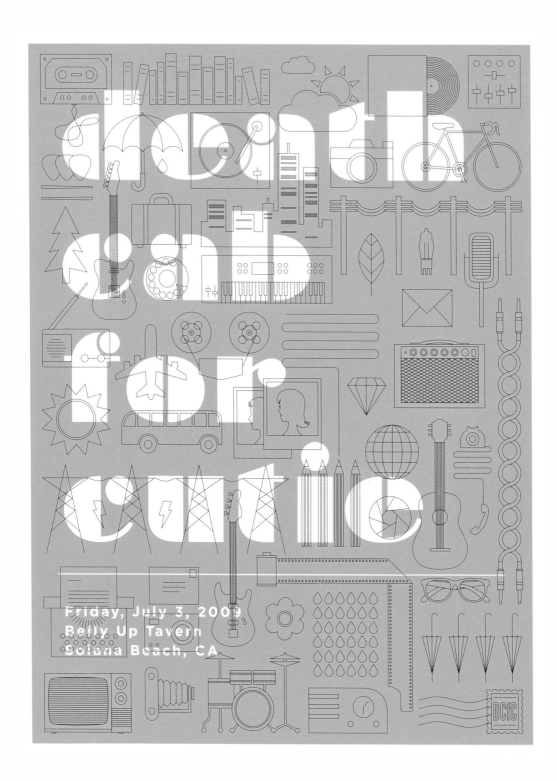

death cab for cutie

Friday, July 3, 2009
Belly Up Tavern
Solana Beach, CA

DEATH CAB FOR CUTIE, 2009
SOLANA BEACH SHOW
Two-color silk screen, 18 × 24 inches

185

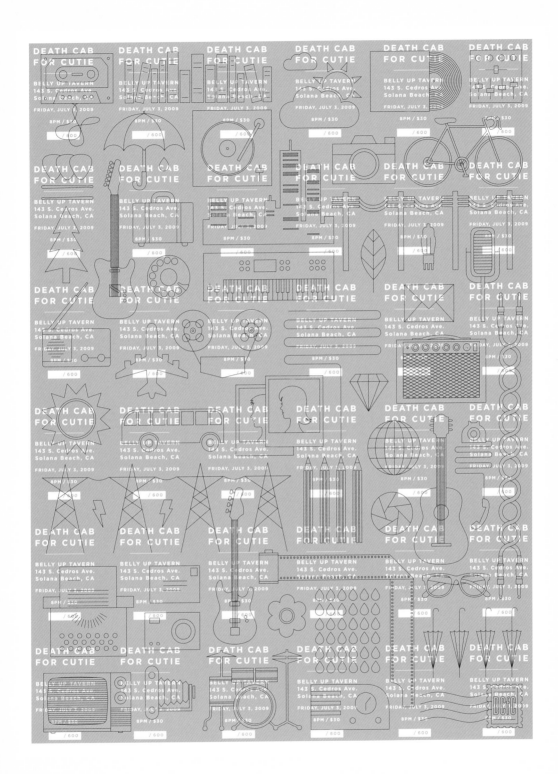

DEATH CAB FOR CUTIE, 2009
UNCUT TICKET SHEET FOR SOLANA BEACH SHOW (Each ticket was hand-numbered.)
Two-color silk screen, 18 x 24 inches

THE DECEMBERISTS, 2009
WITH OTHER LIVES
Three-color silk screen, 18 × 24 inches

Conor Oberst
and the Mystic Valley Band

with Tilly and the Wall / Deep Sea Diver / Michael Runion

Friday, June 26, 2009 / The Anchor Inn / Omaha, NE / 18+

CONOR OBERST AND THE MYSTIC VALLEY BAND, 2009
WITH TILLY AND THE WALL, DEEP SEA DIVER, AND MICHAEL RUNION
Three-color silk screen, 18 × 24 inches

THE SWELL SEASON

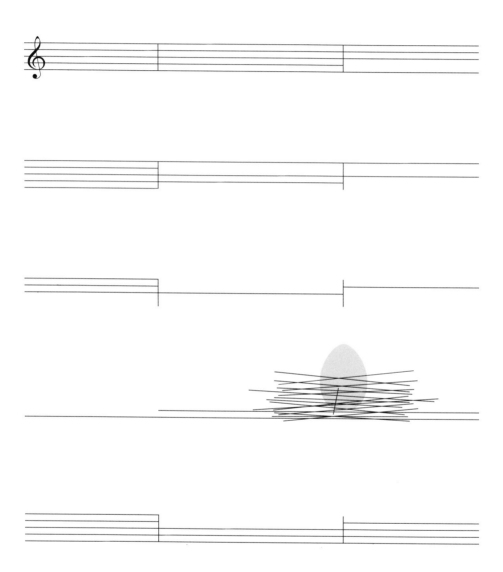

THE SWELL SEASON, 2009
WITH DOVEMAN
Two-color silk screen, 18 x 24 inches

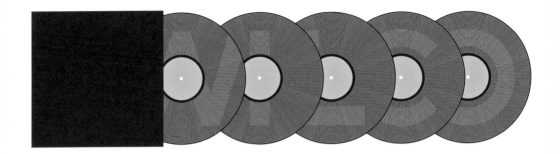

[the album] Wilco (the song) / Deeper Down / One Wing / Bull Black Nova / You And I / You Never Know / Country Disappeared / Solitaire / I'll Fight / Sonny Feeling / Everlasting Everything

WILCO (THE ALBUM), 2009
PROMOTIONAL POSTER
Two-color offset, 35 × 22.75 inches

INDEX